PARENTAL ALIENATION:
quick-read acrostic from an Adult Child Survivor

Endorsed by
~DR. JENNIFER J. HARMAN

Associate Professor, Scientist, world-renowned
& Active Researcher of PARENTAL ALIENATION

Dr. Marni Hill Foderaro

From the award-winning author of the 8-book series
TRUE DECEIT FALSE LOVE

PARENTAL ALIENATION:

quick-read acrostic from an
Adult Child Survivor

Dr. Marni Hill Foderaro

BALBOA.PRESS
A DIVISION OF HAY HOUSE

Balboa Press books may be ordered through booksellers or by contacting:

Balboa Press
A Division of Hay House
1663 Liberty Drive
Bloomington, IN 47403
www.balboapress.com
844-682-1282

Because of the dynamic nature of the Internet, any web addresses or links contained in this book may have changed since publication and may no longer be valid. The views expressed in this work are solely those of the author and do not necessarily reflect the views of the publisher, and the publisher hereby disclaims any responsibility for them.

The author of this book does not dispense medical advice or prescribe the use of any technique as a form of treatment for physical, emotional, or medical problems without the advice of a physician, either directly or indirectly. The intent of the author is only to offer information of a general nature to help you in your quest for emotional and spiritual well-being. In the event you use any of the information in this book for yourself, which is your constitutional right, the author and the publisher assume no responsibility for your actions.

Any people depicted in stock imagery provided by Getty Images are models, and such images are being used for illustrative purposes only. Certain stock imagery © Getty Images.

Print information available on the last page.

ISBN: 979-8-7652-5550-6 (sc)
ISBN: 979-8-7652-5549-0 (e)

Balboa Press rev. date: 09/20/2024

CONTENTS

ENDORSEMENT

"Marni Hill Foderaro's work represents a creative form of expression for the abuse she suffered as a child who had been alienated from a parent by another parental figure. The experience of this form of child abuse is often severe and difficult to process. Books such as this provide insight to this process and have the potential to touch many other adults who were alienated as children and may not be aware they had been abused."

*~**Dr. Jennifer J. Harman,***

Associate Professor, Department of Psychology, Colorado State University, Scientist, World-Renowned & Active Researcher of PARENTAL ALIENATION

DISCLAIMER

DEDICATION

This book is lovingly dedicated to my mom

Elizabeth Ann Hill-Waldenmaier Hansen

My mother passed away in 1996 in her mid-60's, a year after I gave birth to our daughter; this very smart, strong, creative and loving Granni unfortunately never met her only granddaughter. I was slow to put the pieces of my family's Alienation puzzle together. It wasn't until after enduring significant betrayal from those I loved and trusted, experiencing covert Intimate Partner Violence and becoming a severely Targeted Parent that I was fully aware of the Intergenerational component to this extreme form of Child Abuse. It took me until my 60's to figure it all out.

Both my mom and I were teachers, and we both understood that learning takes time and only happens when the student is ready. As long as I could remember, my mom regularly told me that I must be "God's favorite pupil with the scholar sun shining on me" because I often seemed to learn life's lessons the hard way. Well, Mama, I understand now. I'm sorry that I broke your heart by unjustifiably fearing, hating and rejecting you. I was an Alienated Child and was Brainwashed with a False Narrative. Sadly, it's too late for me to ask you for forgiveness and make amends. I do believe you are watching over me from Heaven.

Parental Alienation is a devastating form of Child Psychological Abuse, and Alienated Children should not be blamed for the terrible things they said or did to their Loving Parent; they were in survival mode while they were being used as punishing weapons in the Alienating Parent's war of revenge. However, as much as the Abusers try, the bonds between truly Loving Parents and their Innocent Children can never be severed.

So many wonderful memories of my mom, that were previously blocked, have returned. Her wise and witty "MOTHERWORDS" make so much sense now. Because Alienators and their regime of loyal enablers are so extremely dishonest, use Law Fare and Silver Bullet tactics, create a False Narrative and rewrite history by discarding photos, mementos, gifts, family heirlooms and interfering with all forms of communications, so many children forget the wonderful times shared with their Erased Parent. It is because of this that the final volume of my 8-book series (which is orange-my mom's all-time favorite color) is devoted to the many memories I shared with our two children and is entitled:

TRUE LOVE:
Parental Alienation Cannot Erase the
Many Memorable Moments of a Mother's
TRUE LOVE For Her Children

Happy Mother's Day

Marni Foderaro
& her MOM
Elizabeth Hansen

I was alienated from my late mom from childhood to adulthood, and because the Intergenerational Family Trauma and Abuse Cycle continued, I have chosen to break the chain. I understand now, after studying the research on Parental Alienation and Intimate Partner Violence, the tactics Abusers (and their regime of loyal enablers) use to Coercively-Control, Isolate and Brainwash Young/Adult Children to fear, hate, reject and cut off their Loving, Normal-Range, Targeted Parent. Abusers' masks slip and they often accidentally tell on themselves and expose their malevolent intentions; the shocking secrets and incriminating facts that Alienated Children may find out, might be revealed in a "catalyst event" which would be an instant game changer for them, just as it was for me. Children might question why one parent, seemingly out-of-the-blue, chose to divorce the other after decades of marriage. Hopefully, those close to the Alienated Kids will question this, and when the Alienated Adult Children are emotionally ready, they will begin to connect-the-dots and the truth will be revealed. Targeted Parents who love their children unconditionally would never interfere with their children having a relationship with their other parent because they know children need and should have BOTH parents in their lives. Targeted Parents would always welcome their Alienated Children back with open arms.

Mom, thank you for giving me life and
always loving me unconditionally.

**Mama, your daughter Marnoola-Moo
loves you forever and always.**

"A Mother's gift to her daughter sometimes comes before its time, but its time will come as long as love and laughter light its way.

Will there be love and understanding, or will the lack of acceptance and compassion continue on?"

~Elizabeth Ann Hill-Waldenmaier Hansen

(Born 9-29-1929 Transitioned 9-21-1996)

"MOTHERWORDS" 1990 letter excerpt
to daughter Marni from her Mama

AUTHOR BIOGRAPHY

www.GodCameToMyGarageSale.com

www.amazon.com/author/drmarnihillfoderaro

Dr. Marni Hill Foderaro, loving mother of two wonderful grown children, is both an Adult Child Survivor and severely Targeted Mom of Parental Alienation. She is also an award-winning educator and the best-selling author of the prominently-endorsed 8-book series: "*True Deceit False Love*" which creatively addresses and provides tools, terminology and resources for understanding and healing from Parental Alienation and the Intergenerational Family Trauma that comes with surviving familial/marital Domestic Violence and Narcissistic Abuse. Her latest book: "***PARENTAL ALIENATION: quick-read acrostic from an Adult Child Survivor,***" endorsed by Dr. Jennifer J. Harman, Associate Professor, Scientist, world-renowned and Active Researcher of Parental Alienation, gives a concise overview of how children are weaponized and brainwashed by the Pathogenic, Character-Disordered Parent to reject, fear, hate and cut off their Loving, Normal-Range, Targeted Parent. Marni earned her doctorate in education from Northern Illinois University and completed postdoctoral studies at Harvard during a very successful and rewarding 35-year career as a high school special education teacher, with 12 years as a university graduate school adjunct professor. Marni's life was forever changed after experiencing numerous trauma-induced STEs-Spiritually Transformative Encounters. Her 2022 Hollywood Book Fest runner-up, 2020 Best Books finalist Award Winning and 5-Star Reader's Favorite Spiritual fiction, inspired by true events: "***God Came To My Garage Sale***" is prominently endorsed by James Redfield, best selling author of "*The Celestine Prophecy*" series of books and other notables in the Spiritual community, including founding directors of IANDS-International Association for Near Death Studies. In addition to her TV/podcast interviews, speaking engagements and various writing endeavors, Marni is a contributing author to numerous anthology books. In 2022 Dr. Marni Hill Foderaro was inducted into the Bestselling Authors International (BAI) Organization. Marni was born in the South, raised her children in the Midwest and lives in the Caribbean. She is a lover of animals, nature, music and world travel who handles life's challenges with love, compassion, forgiveness and positivity. She values honesty, integrity, equality and goodness and prays for peace on earth and understanding within our families. Marni believes that truth eventually prevails over lies, and that no Young/Adult Child deserves to experience the extreme Abuse of Parental Alienation.

P- ARENTAL ALIENATION does not just happen to young kids; this form of child abuse can happen to adult children too. Parental Alienation is when a child, without any true reason or justification, completely turns against one of their parents, as a result of covert psychological abuse and manipulation from their other parent, and their many loyal enablers. There are many of us adult child survivors of Parental Alienation who now realize that one of our own parents gaslit us kids and taught us to unjustifiably hate, fear and reject our other loving parent. Being brainwashed, told outright lies and believable half-truths so we would take sides and align with the alienating parent, often happened around the time of our parents' divorce. When the alienating parent conducted a smear campaign and enlisted our friends, our friends' parents, neighbors, teachers, other professionals and even our extended family to believe bad things about our targeted parent, they manipulated them to believe their false narrative and dishonest version of the facts. Alienators crave external validation and are overly concerned about their public image, wanting others to see them as upstanding members in the community. They don't care about how their actions hurt us kids. They played the victim card, wanting sympathy, admiration and to appear that they were the best parent ever. Their narcissistic supply ran dry, and to save face, they used and abused their own children in their obsessive war of revenge.

A- DULT CHILDREN can be weaponized and are vindictively used by the alienating, favored parent we are aligned with to get back at our other parent because they learned the truth about their dishonest, immoral or illegal behavior, and then had the courage to escape. It doesn't matter that we had positive experiences growing up and have great childhood memories of the parent we cut out of our lives; the alienator has subtle, covert tactics to get us to question reality. We go through cognitive dissonance as we experience underhanded gaslighting. We are told "that didn't happen" or "you didn't see or hear what you thought you did" or "you are misinterpreting those past events." They may even tell you that your memory is and has always been poor, even though that was never the case before. This causes us children to doubt our own eyes and ears. The alienator will also discard photos, scrapbooks, mementos, family heirlooms, gifts and intercept communications from the targeted parent so there's no tangible evidence of their presence or love for their kids. They will block the other parent's phone number and email from our own phone without us knowing. Because the alienator often pays for the phone/computer plans and gives us Air Tags, they continuously monitor all of our communications, searches and subscriptions while they are tracking our whereabouts to know where we go and who we see. The stress leads to self-doubt and insecurities, drawing us closer to our favored "good" parent and further away from our rejected "bad" parent, especially if this gaslighting is reinforced and echoed by others in our circle. We often go through bouts of depression, anxiety and panic attacks. We end up believing the lies and start to accuse our "bad" parent for things that we've been told about them that they did or didn't do, even though our lived experience doesn't support these claims. We begin to absorb the false narrative created by our abusing alienator.

R- ED FLAGS which could alert us that something is just not right, are ignored because our memories have been rewritten by our alienating parent. Parental Alienation is solidified if our loving, normal-range, targeted parent is removed from our daily lives. Alienators will go to great lengths to separate us from and erase our other parent, and sometimes our siblings. They will have them arrested on false charges, use the silver bullet strategy with law fare to destroy them financially, tarnish their positive reputation and credibility, ensure they lose their jobs along with their support system, file unwarranted restraining orders, misreport and lie about abuse or mental health to have them taken away for psychological evaluations and placement, abduct the kids and move them across town or to another state or country, change their name and these days may even change their gender without the other parent's consent or input. Alienators commonly violate court orders, interfere with custody and parenting time and in some horrific cases, we kids lose our loving parent to the ultimate separation: death. Our loving parent may be so abused and despondent that they commit suicide because they can't imagine life without their kids, have lost everything and don't see any hope for justice. Some alienators commit murder of our other parent or have them murdered by proxy, many also killing the kids. Alienators are very calculating and may be involved in coordinating some unsuspecting, unfortunate "accident." If our targeted parent is un-alived, we kids may feel we have no choice but to fully align with the only parent we have left. Unfortunately, we may go through our lifetimes without ever knowing the full story or truth.

E- MOTIONAL TRAUMA of erasing half our DNA forever alters us both as a child and adult. Our alienator coerces us to reject our other parent under concern "for our safety and well being", then usually we also cut off that entire side of our family. Relationships we once enjoyed with grandparents, aunts, uncles and cousins are no longer. We align so deeply, becoming loyal only to our favored parent, experience Stockholm Syndrome and are trauma-bonded to our "captor." We're sympathetic to the only parent we think loves us and is protecting us from harm. We don't see their strategy at play or realize that we're slowly being isolated while we're going through it. We trust our alienator and truly believe that we're doing the right thing by choosing to reject our other parent. We experience Cognitive Dissonance, the uncomfortable and stressful feeling that we know that something is wrong or doesn't make sense, but we are made to believe that it is right. An example could be that what one parent tells me about the other is very different than my own experience that I have had directly with them, yet I am forced to go along with a False Narrative against my own better judgment. The emotional trauma plays out during our entire lifetimes with regards to our own self-worth, coping skills, addictions, ability to maintain financial and emotional independence, as well as establish positive relationships and interact appropriately with others.

N- ARCISSIST, PSYCHOPATH, SOCIOPATH and other cluster B personality/character disordered abusers describe the undiagnosed traits of our alienating parent, even though they put down others and claim that they are above others in every way. These abusers all seem to follow the same playbook using projection to accuse our loving parent of the bad behaviors that they themselves are actually doing. Our parents may have been in marriage counseling and even included us kids in family therapy sessions, but the diagnosis given by the "expert" psychologist was usually assigned to the wrong parent. Our alienator can somehow convince others that there's nothing wrong with them. They never admit fault or take responsibility for their wrongdoing, and certainly never acknowledge their role in contributing to the alienation of us children. They blame-shift, deflect and point fingers at others. False accusations have serious consequences leading to false arrests, damaging permanent records, loss of freedoms, homes and assets, separation of our siblings and removal of one of our parents from our lives. It's hard for kids to process all of this; we aren't developmentally capable of understanding what's happening. The trauma cuts like a knife, deep into our soul, yet we don't have the words, experience or support to process our confusion and emotional pain.

T- AUGHT TO HATE, that's the brainwashing goal of our alienating parent. They want us to turn on our other parent. Children naturally love, depend on and want both their dad and mom in their lives. Research shows that ONLY in cases of Parental Alienation (NOT true abuse) do you see a child completely reject, hate, fear and cut off one of their parents. The alienation occurs under the radar so the alienator's abuse isn't obvious. What the alienating parent doesn't realize is that they're really hurting us kids. Why can't they love US more than they hate our other parent? Why doesn't our alienator prioritize OUR well-being? Whatever happened to doing what is BEST FOR THE CHILDREN? Kids are filled with shame, hurt and anger. We just want a peaceful home; it's tough enough navigating life as it is. We end up walking on eggshells waiting for the next shoe to drop. Nobody takes the time to communicate with us kids and process what's going on. It's easy for us to become emotionally unstable, paranoid, physically sick, needy and anxious. We struggle with low self-esteem, forming positive relationships, setting healthy boundaries and choosing friends/partners who aren't abusive. We develop issues with self-worthiness, autoimmune diseases, suicide ideation, eating disorders, substance abuse and a wide array of addictions. The damaging consequences are significant and lifelong.

A- LIGNING with our favored parent is the only way we can survive in our altered family system. It's easier to unjustifiably reject our loving parent than it is to face the uncertain punishing wrath of not falling in line with our alienator. The targeted parent we now cut off was the parent who was always there for us and encouraged us to be our own independent person, take on and follow through with responsibilities and pursue our own interests. Our alienating parent has our life already planned out for us and either wanted us to become their mini-me extension of who they were (or failed to be) or they inappropriately wanted us to be their sympathizer, counselor or servant. The alienator ensures that we'll always be dependent on them financially and emotionally, long into adulthood, with conditional strings attached. They don't want us to be able to think independently, so we second guess ourselves, always feeling subservient, needing approval or permission for even basic decisions. Many alienated children grew up unable to keep a steady job, maintain our health, form positive relationships and make it on our own. That's the alienator's sick, destructive plan because then they can blame our failure to thrive on our other parent.

L- OST, ABANDONED CHILD is what we become. First we aligned with our alienating parent, cutting off our previously loving relationship with our targeted parent, losing half of who we are. Then, as we got older and started to put the pieces of the puzzle together, we realized that we unjustifiably rejected and hurt our loving parent, even referring to them by their first name, and not "dad" or "mom." Adult child survivors of PA feel scared to right this wrong, but hopefully more of us will muster up the courage to reach back out to our targeted parent. Realizing we've been a product of alienation takes decades. A catalyst to our awareness is having our own children and experiencing losing them to alienation from our abusive ex. It's often in midlife when we see the complete picture and realize that there is an intergenerational component to Parental Alienation. We eventually end up experiencing the loss of both parents: first the parent we rejected due to alienation, then our self-preservation need to go low/no-contact with our abusive alienator because we learned the truth and can no longer just go along to get along after knowing their role in the alienation. We kids eventually experience the death of both of our living parents, just at different times in our lives. We now have CPTSD, and have trouble dealing with our body's adrenaline fight or flight responses.

A- TTACHMENT-BASED issues in children result from losing the natural and healthy bond with our loving, safe, normal-range, available parent. We experience psychological splitting once we are conditioned to favor our emotionally abusive, alienating parent. Our alienator (under the guise of care and concern) acts like they are protecting us from harm, which then creates a child-victim narrative with lies and implanted false memories. This causes us to reject our loving parent, which takes years to overcome, if ever. Lives are forever altered by just one malevolent, selfish abuser with a misguided agenda. Identification and treatment of our abuser is possible, however the alienating parent never sees the destruction they cause, take ownership or admit to their bad behavior. The much-needed early intervention of this child psychological abuse just doesn't usually happen, and is in fact perpetuated by others who support the alienator, including "experts" and other professionals (lawyers, judges, GALs, teachers, pastors, counselors, coaches, doctors, etc...) because some are sadly part of the corrupt system, while others are simply unaware or uneducated regarding the nuanced behaviors associated with Parental Alienation.

L- IES AND LEGAL ABUSE are typical with Parental Alienators. Not only is our alienating parent dishonest and misuses the judicial system, they enlist US, the innocent children, in doing the same. The aligned kids are trained to lie and go along with the false narrative and campaign of denigration against our unsuspecting parent, the parent who loves us kids unconditionally and didn't ever expect us to take sides and turn on them. In some cases, when we're no longer minors and become legal adults, our alienator will force us to lie in court or on legal documents to support their false narrative. In severe cases, adult children may be coached to engage in our own law fare and take out restraining orders on our own loving, targeted parent. Judges, lawyers and the family courts wrongly contribute to PA, tearing families apart by favoring the abusers, who act calm, cool and collected and have the money, connections and motivation to continue abusing this system. Alienators feel they are above the law and don't honor court/custody orders or shared parenting arrangements.

I- NDEPENDENT THINKER PHENOMENON happens to most of us children who become alienated. We're so conditioned and brainwashed. Our alienator acts like a cult leader, grooming their unsuspecting followers, by using similar tactics of isolation and coercive control. They're the predator and we're the prey. When children all of a sudden reject one parent, even though there were no prior issues before the divorce, that's an alienation red flag. Actually, the alienation and smear campaign of our loving parent was many years in the making, even though it appears to come out of nowhere and only after our family fell apart. While it's happening, we feel that rejecting and cutting off our targeted parent is our decision, and ours alone. We justify our actions by stating we fear and hate them for what they did to us, even if we can't site firsthand examples to truly justify such an extreme response. We vehemently defend our preferred parent and profess that they had absolutely no influence in the rejection. It takes years for the truth to be revealed that we were negatively influenced and used by one parent to get back at the other parent.

E- NMESHMENT happened with the parent we thought was protecting us from harm. We didn't realize that we became over-involved with our alienating parent. Our alienator's divide-and-conquer strategy blended our boundaries so we were sucked into their drama and destruction. Children are supposed to have their own identities and develop autonomy; well, not when there's PA at play. This imbalance (parentification) is all-consuming where we become overly concerned with our parent's emotional well-being, when that shouldn't be our concern; it should be the other way around. We're just kids. We want to live a happy life like we see our neighborhood pals or classmates enjoy. We begin to experience all-or-nothing, black-and-white-thinking. Since we feel responsible for our alienator's happiness, we set aside our own needs and become silent shadows. We internalize that our feelings and needs should take a back seat to others', so we people-please, over-give and accept (and even come to expect) poor treatment from others.

N- EGATIVE COPING SKILLS were the result of enduring Parental Alienation in childhood. We developed the pattern of constantly seeking acceptance and validation from outside sources, as opposed to trusting our own gut intuition and internal compass. We strive to keep the peace, and that means keeping quiet and not upsetting the apple cart with our own needs. All we want is love and stability, which we no longer have within our family unit. For our survival, many of us had to grow up fast and escaped our home life at an early age. After losing our targeted parent, we lacked consistent positive role models, we find ourselves in toxic relationships and have normalized poor treatment from others. We ignore issues that we should address and find unhealthy ways to cope. Alienated children tend to ruminate, replaying events over and over; the result is re-traumatizing ourselves. We cope in unhealthy ways, including addictions, self-sabotage and seeking unhealthy relationships, and must learn to make our emotional, physical and spiritual health a priority moving forward.

A- UTHORITIES are uninformed about and contribute to PA. Families are being torn apart, not just from the alienating parent, but the collective abuse that is perpetuated by countless others. The alienator goes to extremes to discredit the targeted parent with their smear campaign, isolation tactics and continued intimate partner violence. What many of us kids fail to see is that our alienator is also conducting a covert smear campaign on US so that WE are discredited. Why would they do that to their own children? Because they know that someday we may find out the truth, confront/step away from them and expose the alienator for the evil, abusive person they are. Our alienator wants us to stay loyal, keeping up their false narrative. Subconsciously, they have their own deep-rooted shame and fear of abandonment. They revel that we have gone along with them, and it brings them great satisfaction that we have rejected our other parent. Our alienator wants us to fail in life, which may seem counterintuitive. They want us to struggle with our relationships and jobs because they don't want us to be independent or experience self-made success. They also want to blame our failings on our other parent. They want us mentally ill (like they mislabeled our healthy, loving parent) and will encourage us to be admitted for psych hospitalizations. We need to open our eyes to the motivation and actions of our alienating parent, the lengths they will go to use us for revenge and the authorities they enlist to carryout their misguided mission.

T- RAUMA BONDING, TRIANGULATION AND VIRTUE SIGNALING are all factors adult child survivors of PA face. Children become trauma-bonded when we're emotionally tied to our alienator, forming an unhealthy destructive parent-child relationship. We become psychologically dependent on our alienator, as they're very skilled in bread-crumbing and their use of intermittent reinforcement with a cycle of positive rewards and negative punishment. We children are secretly triangulated when our alienator uses this manipulation strategy to exploit us regarding our interactions with and feelings about our targeted parent. Their goal is to divide-and-conquer. Conflicts are exacerbated and communications are misunderstood, which serve to control and divert attention from the truth. Virtue signaling involves the alienator wearing the narcissistic mask to fool everyone around them to believe they're ethical, good-intentioned, caring, morally superior and have integrity. They're overly concerned with their outward appearance, even though they treat their family, and us children, poorly behind closed doors.

I- NTERMITTENT REINFORCEMENT, INVALIDATION, INJUSTICE AND ISOLATION are all factors our alienating abuser uses to keep us in check, mixing positives and negatives to keep us strung along. They don't truly care about the damage they do to us children, because in their agenda to destroy our other parent, the ends justify the means. Our targeted parent learns about injustice, and we kids learn that life is not fair. When our alienator isolates us and covertly takes away our relationship with our other parent, along with their side of the family (often times for many years-even decades) they are damaging our lives forever. The alienator also uses the divide-and-conquer method with our siblings, often encouraging extreme sibling rivalry and separating us from each other so we don't compare notes about the terrible treatment from our alienator, or their secret immoral/illegal behavior or the true version of our relationship with the parent we are wrongly rejecting. Alienators do this to keep up the false narrative. We feel the heartache of so much time lost and the participatory guilt of so many milestones missed. Our childhood has been hijacked and because of Parental Alienation, and our adulthood has been forever altered.

O- RDERS OF PROTECTION unjustly issued, returning or discarding gifts and letters from our targeted parent, intercepting communications, throwing away photos and family heirlooms, violating court recommendations, changing names or secretly moving us far away are just some of the many actions our alienating parent does to interfere with our previously healthy and loving relationship with our now-targeted parent. Parental Alienation is a severe form of child abuse, Our abusers want to make sure that after the alienation is underway, we cannot reconnect, recover, rebuild, reunite or reconcile with the parent that we no longer have, or now even want, in our lives. Parents who love their children unconditionally would never interfere with them having a relationship with their other parent, as they believe (and research shows) that kids need and should have both parents in their lives. Minor children should not be burdened with details of court cases. They should not be lied to or gaslit or made to feel that they are unloved or unwanted by one of their parents. Kids deserve the love of both of their parents, should be free to have them both in their lives and certainly should not be legally separated, especially through false allegations that led to judicial decisions, including orders of protection.

N- EGATIVE INFLUENCES AND OUR NEVER-ENDING NIGHTMARE of surviving family trauma and narcissistic abuse contribute to a lifelong healing journey for adult child survivors of Parental Alienation. It's not just our alienating parent's words and actions that negatively impact us, it's also so many others around us, whether it is a neighbor, babysitter, teacher, coworker, doctor, therapist, church member, sports coach and even our own siblings and extended family. When we hear the same false narrative being echoed by the masses, and if that same narrative is heard repeatedly over a period of time by different people, then we are more apt to internalize the inaccurate messages, which contribute to our faulty programming and belief system, solidifying the Parental Alienation. We have been an innocent victim of abuse, exploited with psychological, emotional, financial and some of us, sexual manipulation, inflicted by a parent who we trusted, but whose intention was to dominate and use us through coercive control. We were weaponized against our targeted parent, and the fallout takes a lifetime to recover from. At least now, more and more adult child survivors of Parental Alienation are investigating the research, questioning their experiences with both of their parents and speaking out to share their stories. We can choose to step away from negative influences and chart our own path towards truth, peace and love.

"When you heal yourself, you heal your lineage.
Your impact will ripple through generations.
The self-work that you do today will impact the way your
children, and their children, and their children, experience
the world.

I see you, cycle breaker. Keep doing the good work."

~Michell C. Clark

Bestselling Author who believes "writing saved his life"

"There can be no keener revelation of a society's soul than the way in which it treats its children."

~Nelson Mandela

South African anti-apartheid activist, politician and Nobel Prize for Peace Medalist

Dr. Marni Hill Foderaro, loving mother to her two wonderful children, award-winning educator and best selling author, wrote this book, as well as the prominently-endorsed 8-book series: ***"TRUE DECEIT FALSE LOVE"*** which creatively addresses Parental Alienation, Domestic Violence, Narcissistic Abuse, Best Friend Betrayal and Intergenerational Family Trauma. In this latest book: ***"PARENTAL ALIENATION: quick-read acrostic from an Adult Child Survivor"*** she speaks from the perspective of an Adult Child Survivor, as opposed to a severely Targeted Mom, although she has experienced both ends of this abusive spectrum. In this quick and easy-to-read acrostic, Marni gives a concise overview of how young and adult children are weaponized, brainwashed, isolated, bought-off and coercively-controlled by the Pathogenic, Character-Disordered, Alienating Parent to reject, fear, hate and cut off their Loving, Normal-Range Targeted Parent.

Marni eventually (finally in her 60's) fully realized that she was an Adult Child Survivor of Parental Alienation ONLY after becoming a severely Targeted Mom. Narcissists are successful in their underhanded efforts to use the Divide-and-Conquer strategy; they are most likely motivated by their need to cover up some significant wrongdoing or immoral/illegal behavior. They want to keep children isolated, even from their own siblings, so that they don't compare notes and find out the truth of what they did.

To understand why such bad things happen to good people, Marni embarked on years of reading the research and doing the inner shadow-work to acknowledge her foundational patterns and take ownership for her role in the family dysfunction. Marni was absolutely shocked and devastated to experience Parental Alienation. In what felt like a blink of an eye, she also lost her home, assets, money and support system of family, friends, neighbors and church. Targeted Parents are forced to grieve the death of their living children, the same way the child grieves the death of their Loving Parent. So many significant milestones and everyday events are missed.

However, Marni is a Loving Mom who is a strong and resilient survivor. She handles betrayal and life's challenges with grace, honesty, compassion, kindness and love. She believes that truth eventually prevails over lies. Marni hopes and prays that Parental Alienation is not a life sentence, but a temporary setback for our loving souls to grow and evolve.

Marni's heartfelt message to
Adult Alienated Children:

We, Adult Child Survivors of severe Parental Alienation, have the power to right the harmful wrongs which have been perpetrated against us. We don't have to accept that one parent is all-good and the other is all-bad; that black-and-white thinking is a clear indicator that we have been taught to hate. We can use our own critical thinking skills, follow our own gut intuition about our own lived experiences, do some in-depth research and honest reflection and find the strength and courage to reach out to our Targeted Parent, the Loving Dad or Loving Mom who we unjustifiably cut out of our lives as a result of Parental Alienation.

Even if it's been years or decades since we last had any contact with our Erased Parent, and we may be afraid or feel guilt and shame for how poorly we treated them, we can take the initiative and begin the process of reconnecting and regaining trust, which is natural after so much time apart. Children deserve to learn what really happened in our family and with our relationship with our dad and mom, as shocking and heartbreaking as it may be. Knowing, understanding and acknowledging the truth that we have experienced Parental Alienation is a more authentic way to live and is essential on our self-actualization and healing journey. Help and support for Alienated Adult Children is still somewhat limited, but now more people are stepping forward as they become aware that they have endured this form of extreme Child Abuse.

Our voices matter. The truth matters.
Goodness matters. Love matters.

It's validating to study the research on Parental Alienation as we connect with and/or hear the stories of others who have experienced what we have gone through, to know that we are not alone. For our own self-preservation and to stay true to our honorable values, we may find we need to set Healthy Boundaries by stepping back from the manipulation to reevaluate our relationships with those who have harmed us, especially our Alienating Parent and the enablers who supported them. We hold the key to unlock and put an end to the Intergenerational Family Trauma Abuse Cycle of Parental Alienation.

Now is the time to heal and live with more love, peace, honesty, compassion, forgiveness and awareness. We need to honor and respect ourselves, be more discerning and reach out to reconnect with our Targeted Parent who we unjustifiably rejected and who has always loved us unconditionally.

www.GodCameToMyGarageSale.com

www.amazon.com/author/drmarnihillfoderaro

PARENTAL ALIENATION
Abuse of a child is
TRUE DECEIT
FALSE LOVE

To the alienating dad or mom:

PLEASE LOVE YOUR CHILD MORE THAN YOU HATE THEIR OTHER PARENT!

From an Adult Child Survivor.

Printed in the United States
by Baker & Taylor Publisher Services